THE JEWISH ADVENTURERS' CLUB

by
"Commodore" Bruce Selitz
Helen "Speed" Merkin
"Sir Edmund" "Mitch" "Nachus,"
"Doctor" Seldom Conroy

illustrations by Dennis Corrigan

A DELL TRADE PAPERBACK

To David Hayward, without whom
the Jewish Adventurers' Club
would never have been born.

ACKNOWLEDGMENTS

We would like to thank the following Adventurers, who helped us
when they weren't busy: Assemblyman Brodsky, Mark Saltzman,
Claudia Schulman, Stuart Himmelfarb, Chaim Brown, Alan
Schwartz, Kathleen Moloney, Glen Waggoner, Pam Woodstein, Cliff
Fagin, Terre Roche, Melissa Haizlip, Jack Korkes, Naomi Merkin,
Esto, Dolly Stiles, Jennifer Lumar, Steve Tanen, Norman Stiles,
Kathy Bishop, Maura Wechsler.

Special thanks to:

Marilyn Abraham and Esther Newberg

A special thanks to the people who helped me create the art in this
book by posing as models: Carl Armideo, Michael Chen, Rebecca
Corrigan, Sara Corrigan, Sue Foster, William Gabrielson, Susan
Gabrielson, Marjorie C. Murphy, Daniel Stott. Loving thanks to
my wife, Donna Pacinelli.

Dennis Corrigan

A DELL TRADE PAPERBACK
Published by
Dell Publishing Co., Inc.
1 Dag Hammarskjold Plaza
New York, New York 10017

Designed by Sheree Goodman

Dell ® TM 681510, Dell Publishing Co., Inc.

ISBN: 0-440-54197-2

Printed in the United States of America

November 1987

10 9 8 7 6 5 4 3 2 1

VB

Who Is This Book For?

Everybody.

Just what do we mean by everybody? Hey, anyone with a dream, or something like that.

Have you ever dared to think about ironing with wet hands? Have you yearned to eat an airport nacho? Do you ever fantasize about giving yourself a haircut? Do you? Huh?

Then you might belong in the Jewish Adventurers' Club.

You don't have to be Jewish. You don't even have to pay dues to be a member, although we prefer it and hope we don't have to bring up the subject again. Simply put, you can be anyone from anywhere who has a burning desire to live life on the edge. If you love thrills, challenge, danger . . . if you're not afraid to talk back to fate . . . if you're ready to risk injury, death, or worse . . . the JAC is for you.

You have nothing to lose except maybe a thumb.

A History of the Jewish Adventurers' Club

riginally, the club was nothing more than a loose-knit, informal, sometime thing. We used to meet every now and then in our leader Chance Weinburg's kitchen. He would call and say, "Hey, you want to do something crazy?" A year later everybody would say, "Okay."

You just couldn't say no to Chance. He was that kind of guy. Only Chance could say "Hey, can I use your comb?"— and mean it. He was our leader. We were the model airplane, and he was the glue. When tragedy struck, we fell apart.

It was July 4, 1984. A sunny day. A beach day. The kind of day where everyone but Chance had a lot of white stuff on his nose.

We were barbecuing (without fluid, but using a short match). People were enjoying themselves. We should have known.

Chance went swimming. *Only half an hour after eating a cookie.*

It wasn't the first time he'd done this. He just did it once too often.

Chance Weinburg played Ping-Pong with death that day and lost—21 to 6.

We were devastated.

Until July 5, 1984, when we formed the Jewish Adventurers' Club, amidst much internal bickering about whether Sir Edmund should be allowed to join.

Why the JAC? As Chance would have said, "Hey, why not?"

Even the most fearless pathfinders need a compass to show them the way. Even the nuttiest daredevils need an occasional safety net. Even the bravest among us sometimes needs a hand to hold, or even a night-light.

And, of course, there is Chance. He is the best reason—the true reason—for the existence of the Jewish Adventurers' Club. Yes, the JAC is our tribute to Chance Weinburg. It is our only way of saying thanks. And most important, it is our attempt to keep his spirit of adventure alive as best we can. When we're not busy.

"Commodore" Bruce Selitz

"Commodore" Bruce Selitz was born in Atlanta, Georgia, to a very old hat-blocking family. An only child, he was the product of a ten-month pregnancy. As a result, he loves anything to do with water—drinking it, bathing in it, sleeping in it. The Commodore is forty-three years old and gained membership in the JAC by riding in a subway with a wet head—without holding on. Allergic to herring and chocolate.

Helen "Speed" Merkin

Helen "Speed" Merkin developed a fondness for oak tag during a sixteen-year bout with mono. She still doesn't know why; she just likes the smell. Born in Jerusalem while on tour with the Basie Band, she now resides in Club Meds around the world. She is a charter member of the JAC, having gained membership when she had her legs waxed without local anesthesia. Allergic to mimeograph fluid.

"Sir Edmund"
"Mitch" "Nachus"

"Sir Edmund" "Mitch" "Nachus" became a neatness nut after he was once yelled at by his father for tearing his good pants. His proudest accomplishment is catching a foul ball at a Mets game without breaking his nose. (He later had the ball cleaned and gave it back.) A gym teacher specializing in dodge ball, he's always wanted to live on a houseboat. Sir Edmund was allowed to join the JAC after he claimed to have accepted a ride from a stranger in 1973. His membership is currently in dispute. Allergic to dampness and volleyball netting.

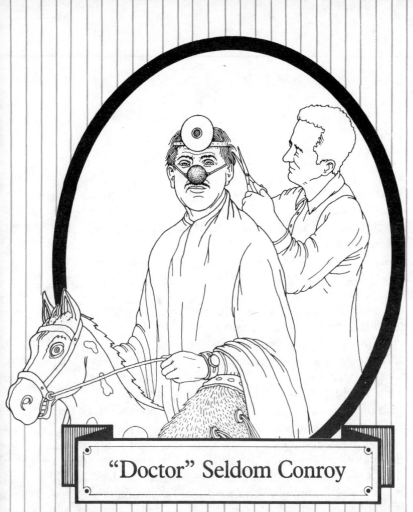

"Doctor" Seldom Conroy

"Doctor" Seldom Conroy, who possesses an unusual respect for the human voice, is the only person from his neighborhood ever jailed for oversleeping. The Doctor was recently granted honorary membership in the JAC after recovering from a stroke he suffered while filling up on bread. He currently works as a clown in the Norwegian Rodeo. Allergic to Sir Edmund.

What Is a Jewish Adventurer?

After much serious study, thought, and discussion, we have haphazardly decided that there are four basic types of Jewish Adventurer: Novice, Advanced, Daredevil, and Crazy Person.

Each category denotes a level of expertise and also serves as a fairly accurate indication of a specific Adventure's level of risk.

To serve future Adventurers, we have prepared a handy chart that will help define and explain the different degrees of danger. As you examine the chart, observe your own reactions to the Adventures listed. Don't worry if anything past Novice makes you break out in a cold sweat. It's normal. Just relax, put on a warm sweater, and keep reading till you break through the wall. Never forget that we're here to lead you by the hand, to take you gently up the folding stepladder of high risk. If it seems impossible that you'll ever reach the exalted rung that belongs only to the Crazy Person, you might be right. But we don't think so. Just the fact that you've read this far means you've got what it takes. It'll take nerve, it'll take hard work, and it'll take plenty of rest. But we think you can do it.

Start now.

Sit down, make sure both feet are on the floor, and learn what adventure is all about.

A HANDY CHART

CLASSIFICATION	NON-JAC EQUIVALENT	JAC ADVENTURE
Novice	Mountain Climbing	Taking a Shower with a Cold
Advanced	Putting Out an Oil Fire	Not Using Your Phone Machine to Screen Calls
Daredevil	Wingwalking	Going Out with a Wet Head
Crazy Person	Brahma Bull Riding	Drinking Out of a Stranger's Glass

Is it beginning to make sense? Are you starting to feel the blood coursing through your veins?

Hold tight. You're still not ready to begin. Before action there must be learning. You're not ready to let a stiff breeze whistle past your undried hair until you study the history of the JAC and its founding family.

9

○ **CHANCE WEINBURG** ○

10

A Profile of Our Leader
Chance Weinburg

Born: December 25, 1950

Real Name: Andrew Sol Weinburg

Died: July 4, 1984

Cause of Death: Went swimming less than an hour after eating a cookie

Last Words: "Oh yeah? Watch this! If you're not busy."

Mother's Reaction to Death: "See?"

Height: 5'8½"

Shoe Size: 9E

Eye Color: Brownish

Hair Color: Brownish

Favorite Color: Brownish

Education: Brown University (two years)

Disabilities: Color blindness

Awards: Good Neighbor Award for directing traffic during a brownout

Favorite Hat: Cowboy with ear flaps

Favorite Drink: Triple-strength seltzer

Instrument Played: Conga drum

Profession: District sales manager for a major zipper company

Hobbies: Moped racing; collecting versions of "Feelings"

Favorite Song: "Feelings"

Favorite Poet: Leonard Nimoy

Favorite Book: *The Secret of the Caves* by Franklin W. Dixon

Children: None. He and his wife were too busy living life to the fullest

Favorite Actress: Sophia Loren in *Boy on a Dolphin*

Favorite Actor: Martin Milner

Last Wish: That Martin Milner and Sophia Loren would work together

Allergies: Dacron, wool, polyester, and cotton

A Profile of Our Leader's Wife
Renée Weinburg

Born: April 1, 1952

Real Name: Renée Weinburg

Maiden Name: Renée Wyneberg

Married: March 21, 1970

Remarried: Labor Day, 1984

New Husband: Len Wineburg, DDS, PC—a nice, steady man and a good provider

Quote: "Please. Not now. I'm living in Phoenix and loving it. Call me when Len leaves for the office."

Hobbies: Learning to live like a normal person again; collecting luggage

Cause of death: None, yet

Profession: Real estate (also, designing jewelry)

Education: Lemonjello School of Beauté (graduated with highest honors)

Height: 5'4"

Shoe Size: 6B

Favorite Color: White

Favorite Book: Parts of *Smart Women, Foolish Choices* Parts of *Lucky*

Favorite Movie: *The Chosen*

Favorite Actor: Robbie Benson

Favorite Actress: Sophia Loren

Life's Wish: That Robbie Benson and Sophia Loren would work together

Greatest Joy in Life: Getting a nail wrap

Favorite Food: Macaroons

Favorite Drink: Whiskey Sour–Lite

Allergies: Leather, vinyl, and plastic

RENÉE WEINBURG

How to Become
a Member of the
Jewish Adventurers' Club

Your Adventure is about to begin.

But with freedom comes responsibility. And a group as dedicated to risk and danger as the JAC comes with a set of rules. It's our club—so they're our rules. Follow them, and you, too, may one day walk through the portals of the Jewish Adventurers' Club.

To join the club:

1. You must experience at least one of the Adventures described in this book, or its authorized equivalent. (*Note:* You must perform the Adventure *yourself*. Watching someone else does not qualify you for the club.)

2. Sign the card enclosed at the back of the book and put it in your wallet.★

3. If you lose the card, you have to buy the book again.

★If your Adventure is "Carrying Money Loose Without Using a Wallet," you may put the card in your pocket.

How to Be a
Jewish Adventurer

At last!

Welcome to the world of danger.

In the following pages lie the tools and methods of a realm where few have dared to tread.

These Adventures are meant to serve as a guide. They are meant to instruct. Follow them, experience them, and you will change the entire texture and fabric of your life. You will experience that special high that comes from living on the edge.

Not all of the Adventures carry equal weight. Please pay special attention to the classifications Novice, Advanced, Daredevil, and Crazy Person. The classifications are not just for convenience but are safety guidelines that *must* be observed. Do not try any of the Daredevil or Crazy Person Adventures until you have mastered Novice and Advanced. We also strongly suggest getting your booster shots, along with a complete physical, including a full GI series.

14

Adventures in the Great Outdoors

- Leaving the House While Wearing a Bathrobe and Slippers

  Novice: To Get the Paper on Your Own Front Lawn
  Advanced: To Drive Your Spouse to the Train or Your Children to School
  Daredevil: To Mail a Letter at the Corner Mailbox
  Crazy Person: To Go to the Supermarket

- Walking on Cobblestones
- Going on an Overnight Trip Anytime, Anywhere, Without Bringing Contact Lens Rinse, Tampons, Pads, or Blow Dryer

Adventures in Hiking

Novice: Taking a Hike Without a Flashlight
Daredevil: Taking a Hike Without a Flashlight—at Night
Crazy Person: Taking a Hike Without a Canteen

Adventure in Wildlife

Crazy Person: Touching a Bird

- Wearing Socks and Shoes on the Beach (*Possible Hazards:* Hormonal Imbalance, Overheating of the Gonads, and Possible Infertility)

17

Adventures in Wildlife

Novice:
Petting a Dog
That's Not on
a Leash

Advanced:
Petting a
Dog That's
Drooling

Daredevil:
Kissing a
Dog or
Cat

Crazy Person: Kissing
a Dog or Cat on the
Mouth

Kissing a Dog or Cat That's Drooling on the Mouth
(See: "Things We Never Do")

- Wearing Curlers During a Thunder or Lightning Storm
- Walking on Snow or Ice

    Advanced: With Your Hands in Your Pockets
    Daredevil: Running
    Crazy Person: With One Eye Closed

- Asking a Stranger for the Time

Adventures in Wildlife

Novice: Fishing from a Dock
Advanced: Using Worms
Daredevil: Digging for the Worms Yourself
Crazy Person: Storing the Worms in Your Refrigerator Overnight

- Playing on a Seesaw with a Stranger

    Potential Hazards: He or She Might Jump Off at Any Time and Catapult You to Certain Death. Also Leads to Infertility.

- Playing Softball in Your Good Pants
- Walking on the Wrong Side of the Road

Adventure in Jaywalking

Advanced: Jaywalking in Beverly Hills

- Wearing a Short Jacket Outdoors in Wintertime
- Going to an Amusement Park and Standing Near a Roller Coaster or Ferris Wheel
- Going Outside from November to May Without Chap Stick
- Watching a Parade from a Tall Building
- Trailing Your Hand in the Water from Inside a Boat

    Warning: Can Lead to Loss of Limb or Severe Pruning Up

Adventures in Wildlife

Daredevil: Buying a Fur Coat from Someone Who Isn't Related to You
Crazy Person: Not Storing Your Fur Coat During the Summer

- Rolling Down a Hill
- Yelling in a Tunnel
- Running in New Shoes
- Going Down an Alley

Crazy Person: Going Down an Alley at Night

Adventure in Hitchhiking

Daredevil: Picking Up a Female Hitchhiker
Picking up a Male Hitchhiker (See: "Things We Never Do")

- Carrying a Briefcase and Umbrella in One Hand

Warning: Can Result in Tripping and Falling, Umbrella Puncturing Eyeball, Entering Brain, Causing Instantaneous Death. Or Strained Lower Back.

- Going Out Without a Watch on Purpose

Adventure in Wildlife

Advanced: Swimming in a Body of Water Where You Can See Fish

- Going Outside Without Checking to See If You Have Your Keys
- Wearing a Two-Piece Bathing Suit
- Going Out Without Lipstick
- Going to a Beach Without Using Zinc Oxide on Your Nose

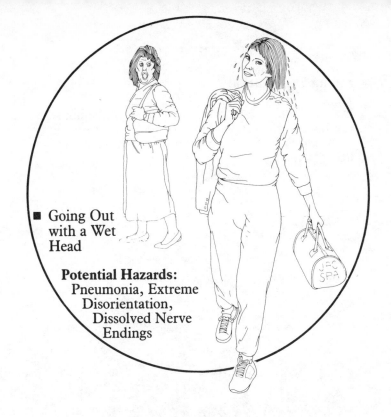

- Going Out with a Wet Head

Potential Hazards:
Pneumonia, Extreme Disorientation, Dissolved Nerve Endings

Adventures in Exploring

(**Note:** We don't consider the basement part of the house; it's considered "outdoors.")

Novice: Going into the Basement in an Unfamiliar House

Advanced: Going into the Basement in an Unfamiliar House—Alone

Daredevil: Going into a Basement Where the Lights Are Broken, with a Flashlight and a Friend

Crazy Person: Going into a Basement Where the Lights Are Broken, Alone, at Night, with a Flashlight

Going into a Basement Where the Lights Are Broken, Alone, at Night, with No Flashlight (See: "Things We Never Do")

Adventures in Food

- Filling Up on Bread

  Instructions: Can be done anywhere—in the home, at the beach, on a train. Don't actually fill up at first; start out with one too many rolls, and work your way up slowly.

Eating Unwashed Fruit (See: "Things We Never Do")

- Drinking Milk out of the Carton
- Ordering a Western Omelet Without Asking What's in It
- Using Your Knife as a Fork (See: "Adventures in Tools")
- Eating Soup Without Blowing on It First
- Eating or Chewing Ice
- Going to Your Grandmother's and Refusing to Eat
- Swallowing Your Gum
- Chewing on a Rubber Band

Eating Fish on the Bone (**Crazy Persons Only!**)

- Touching a Hot Dinner Plate
- Eating with Your Hat On
- Talking and/or Laughing with Your Mouth Full
- Hitting Your Teeth with Your Fork When You Eat
- Sending Your Food Back in a Restaurant
- Eating Raw Hamburger
- Drinking Milk or Orange Juice After the Expiration Date on the Carton
- Putting a Glass on a Table Without Using a Coaster
- Putting Unwrapped Food in Your Pocket and Eating It Later
- Salting Your Food Before Tasting It
- Eating Hot Mustard
- Eating a Lobster Without a Bib
- Opening Up Pistachio Nuts with Your Teeth
- Eating Something That's Fallen on the Floor
- Not Putting a Table Pad Down Under the Tablecloth
- Eating a Snack Before Dinner
- Eating in a Very Dark Restaurant
- Blowing Bubbles in Your Chocolate Milk
- Making Reservations at a Restaurant Under Your Own Name

  (Warning: You must show up or actually cancel if you're planning to eat there again)

- Not Canceling Reservations at a Restaurant

  Asking for MSG at a Chinese Restaurant (See: "Things We Never Do")

Adventures in Champagne

Novice: Standing in the Same Room as Someone Who's Opening a Bottle of Champagne

Advanced: Standing Directly in Back of Someone Who's Opening a Bottle of Champagne

Daredevil: Standing in Front of Someone Who's Opening a Bottle of Champagne

Crazy Person: Opening a Bottle of Champagne Yourself

Adventures in Sex

- Sleeping with an Aerobics Instructor or Wrestler

Adventures in Contraceptives

Novice: Using a Contraceptive Sponge
Advanced: Cleaning Your Kitchen with a Contraceptive Sponge

- Making Noise During an Orgasm
- Wearing Only Your Pajama Bottoms in Bed

Potential Hazards: Frostbite, Severe Exhaustion

- Letting Your Mate Use Your Toothbrush
- Having Sex Anywhere Except in a Bed
- Going on a Blind Date with Someone Named Spike
- Having Sex Without Holding On
- Having Sex While Your Parents Are in the House

Adventures in Getting an Erection

Novice: In an Elevator
Advanced: At a Lecture
Daredevil: On Public Transportation
Crazy Person: Any of the Above on Purpose
Jogging with an Erection (See: "Things We Never Do")

- Having Sex While Giving Blood (Crazy Person Only)
- Oral Sex (Crazy Person Only)
- Wearing Torn or Dirty Underwear on a Date

Adventures in Watching Porn Movies

Novice: With a Date
Advanced: Alone
Daredevil: In the Daytime Without a Hat
Crazy Person: Renting a Porn Movie
Potential Hazards: Whiplash, Bursitis, Amnesia, Frostbite, and Your Name Will Be on Permanent FBI File

Adventures in Having an Orgasm

Novice: One Per Night
Advanced: One Really Good One
Daredevil: Two
Crazy Person: Without Passing Out

- Having Sex with the Light On
- Having Sex with a Friend

Warning: Bring Tape Recorder for Verification of Moment When Friend Says This Will Not Change Relationship

Adventures in Getting a Hickey

Novice: Above the Waist and Below the Chin
Daredevil: Above the Chin
Crazy Person: Anywhere Else

- Giving a Hickey in a Moving Vehicle
- Giving a Hickey to Somebody Taller Than You Are
- *For Women Only:* Having Sex with a Man Shorter Than You Are
- *For Men Only:* Having Sex with a Woman Taller Than You Are

Because It's There—Homage to Bjork and Fish:

All of us have known the experience of being obsessed with the body of another human being and the simple chemistry between two souls that leads them, pushing and squeezing, to an explosion of flesh and fluids that ends in a huge cloud of animal steam. All too familiar, of course—but how familiar was the courage of Jewish adventurers who were the first to ask the question, "What for?"

On April 17, 1957, Karl Bjork, wearing an overheating gauge, was performing a simple Acting Up Maneuver when he experienced a visceral reaction to Christina Fish, who was working with a bread loader. Their coupling—still under dispute as to whether it qualifies as actual sex—was nevertheless a breakthrough. These two heroes charted many miles together, advancing up to, but of course not including, that nearly forbidden and rarely mentioned zone, that of pleasure. How often JAC members recall going into a padded room, strapping themselves in, and listening to a recording of the late Mr. Bjork describing his bedroom adventures as "a good time."

Sexual Adventure Hall of Fame: Fiona Spillane, the first woman to give herself a tracheotomy while performing oral sex and the inventor of the once scorned but now popular Fellatio Mittens.

Suggested Reading:

When the Shaking and the Shouting Stops by Bjork and Fish

Adventures in Shopping

- Bringing More Than Ten Items to a Supermarket Express Checkout Line
- Buying an Electrical Appliance from a Street Vendor
- Going into a Hardware Store
- Walking Up or Down a Moving Escalator Without Holding On (See: "Adventures in Sports"; "Adventures in Travel and Transportation")
- Buying a Used Car from a Newspaper Ad
- Buying a Live Lobster You Intend to Eat Yourself (See: "Adventures in the Great Outdoors")
- Returning Merchandise to a Store Without the Receipt
- Buying Anything with the Label "One Size Fits All"
- Going Shopping Without Your Credit Card

Crazy Person: Not Owning a Credit Card

Adventures in Buying Mail Order

Warning: Not for Novices
Advanced: Without Seeing a Photograph
Daredevil: A Business Suit
Crazy Person: Shoes
Buying Meat (See: "Things We Never Do")

Adventures in Trusting a Salesperson's Opinion

Novice: For a Countertop Appliance
Advanced: For a Stereo
Daredevil: For Clothing
Crazy Person: For Drugs

- Buying Jewelry at an Airport
- Going Shopping the Day Before Christmas
- Buying Antiques
- Going to an Auction

- Buying a Guitar from a Pawnbroker
- Renting Furniture
- Using a Storefront Lawyer or Accountant
- Returning Anything You Bought on Sale

Adventures with the Telephone

Adventures with Your Mother

Novice: Telling Your Mother You Can't Talk to Her Because You're Busy

Advanced: Telling Your Mother You Can't Talk to Her Because There's Someone There

Daredevil: Telling Your Mother You Can't Talk to Her Because There's Someone There—and It's 8:00 in the Morning

Crazy Person: Telling Your Mother You Can't Talk to Her Because There's Someone There and It's 8:00 in the Morning—and You're a Woman

- Answering the Phone with Wet Hands
- Not Using Your Phone Machine to Screen Your Calls
- Cradling the Receiver Between Your Shoulder and Head Without Using Your Hands

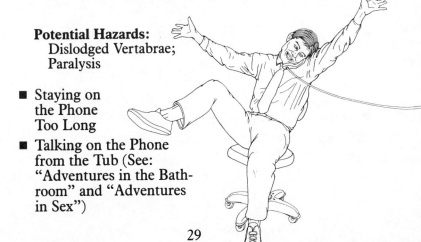

Potential Hazards:
  Dislodged Vertabrae;
  Paralysis

- Staying on the Phone Too Long
- Talking on the Phone from the Tub (See: "Adventures in the Bathroom" and "Adventures in Sex")

29

Adventures in the Bathroom

Adventures in the Wild

Daredevil: Going to the Bathroom Outdoors

Crazy Person: Wiping with Leaves

- Wearing a Sport Jacket on the Toilet
- Showering Without a Mat

- Using European Toilet Paper
- Stepping into a Tub Without Testing the Water First

Shampooing with Your Eyes Open (**Daredevil Only**)

- Throwing Away Q-Tips in the Toilet
- Staying in the Bathtub Too Long
- Not Rotating Your Shampoo and Conditioner

Potential Hazards: Definitely Leads to Baldness

- Going to the Bathroom with the Door Open
- Going to the Bathroom with Nothing to Read
- Going to the Bathroom at a Party When There's No Lock on the Door

Adventures in Shaving

Novice: Shaving Without Having a Styptic Pencil Handy

Advanced: Actually *Using* a Styptic Pencil
(*Warning:* The Painful Sting Could Lead to High Blood Pressure and Eventual Heart Disease)

Daredevil: Shaving Twice in One Day

Crazy Person: Shaving with a Used Blade

Potential Hazards: Blood Poisoning; Maiming; Unintentional Face-Lift

Shaving Without Shaving Cream (See: "Things We Never Do")

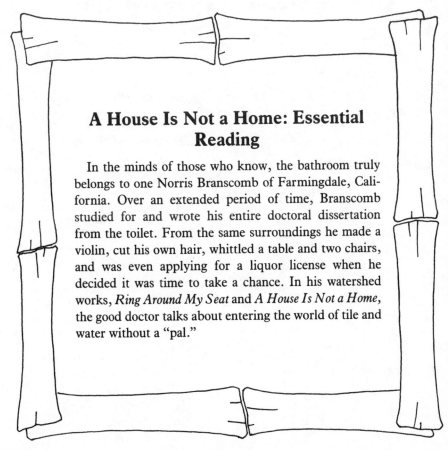

A House Is Not a Home: Essential Reading

In the minds of those who know, the bathroom truly belongs to one Norris Branscomb of Farmingdale, California. Over an extended period of time, Branscomb studied for and wrote his entire doctoral dissertation from the toilet. From the same surroundings he made a violin, cut his own hair, whittled a table and two chairs, and was even applying for a liquor license when he decided it was time to take a chance. In his watershed works, *Ring Around My Seat* and *A House Is Not a Home*, the good doctor talks about entering the world of tile and water without a "pal."

Adventures in Travel and Transportation

- Five in a Cab

  Warning: Do Not Try This Without Proper Medical Supervision

- Riding in a Subway or Bus Without Holding On
- Flying Standby

Adventures in Air Travel

Advanced: Wearing Shorts on an Airplane
Daredevil: Wearing Running Shorts on an Airplane

- Humming in the Car
- Riding an Elevator or Escalator with a Cold
- Trying a New Route to Get Somewhere
- Driving with Your Elbow Resting on the Open Window

Reading in a Moving Vehicle (**Crazy Persons Only!**)

- Speaking French in France

  Advanced: Speaking French in Canada

- Accepting a Ride from a Stranger
- Riding in the Back of a Pickup Truck
- Riding a Bike in Traffic
- Driving a Stick Shift in a Hilly Part of the Country
- Using a Boat to Get Somewhere You Can Reach by Driving

- Driving Past a Gas Station When the Tank Is Less Than Half Full (See: "Adventures in Sports")
- Parking with Your Bumper Touching the Red Zone
- Packing Less Than One Day Before Leaving on a Trip

  Not Taking Extra Underwear and Socks on a Vacation (**Daredevil Only!**)

- Taking a Gypsy Cab
- Leaving Town for More Than Three Days Without the Name of a Local Physician or the Address of the Nearest Hospital

  Crazy Person: Jumping Up and Down in the Backseat of a Parked Car (*Potential Hazard:* Car Will Move, Hit Something Like a Lamppost; You Will Die)

- Sitting on a Subway or Bus Next to Someone Who's Eating

- Asking a Cab Driver for the Best Route to the Airport
- Running in High Heels
- Hopping onto a Boat from a Dock (or Vice Versa) Without Assistance
- Sitting Near the Emergency Exit on a Plane
- Flying with a Head Cold or Ear Infection

Adventures in Sports

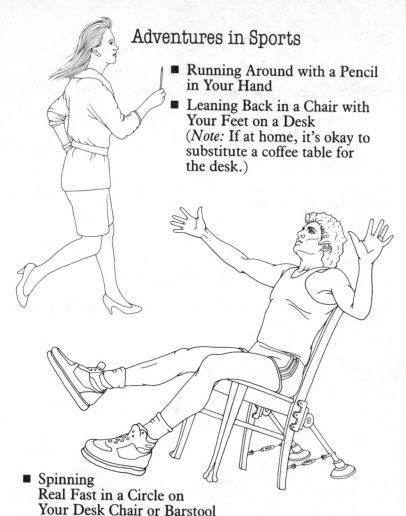

- Running Around with a Pencil in Your Hand
- Leaning Back in a Chair with Your Feet on a Desk
  (*Note:* If at home, it's okay to substitute a coffee table for the desk.)

- Spinning
  Real Fast in a Circle on
  Your Desk Chair or Barstool
- Sitting Around in a Wet Bathing Suit
  (*Note:* World's record held by the late Biffie Lewis. She lasted six days, fourteen hours, and twenty-two minutes.)
- Speed Reading (*Requirement:* Stretch First)
- Buying the Top Newspaper from the Pile
- Playing Ball in the Rain
- Going to Bed Without Setting the Alarm

Adventures in Suburban Sports

Novice: Lighting a Barbecue with a Long Match
Advanced: Using a Short Match
Daredevil: Using Fluid
Crazy Person: Using Fluid *and* a Short Match

- Sliding on Linoleum in Your Socks
  (*Note to Concerned JAC Members:* Start your write-in campaign now! Make this an Olympic Sport by 1992!)
- Running in the House
- Jumping on the Bed
- Fighting with Your Pillow
- Turning On an Electrical Appliance During a Thunder and Lightning Storm

Adventures in Driving in Inclement Weather

Novice: Drizzle
Advanced: Downpour
Daredevil: Snow
Crazy Person: Snow at Night

- Getting Overheated (This can be incorporated into almost every other Adventure. Go for it! But for Pete's sake, see the Overheating Gauge in "The Official JAC Catalog.")
- Getting Overtired
- Almost Getting into a Fight
- Talking to a Policeman
- Shaking Hands with Someone Who's Been to Prison

Adventures in Ear Piercing

Novice: By a Doctor
Advanced: By a Jeweler
Daredevil: By Anyone Else
Crazy Person: By Yourself

Adventures in Using Someone Else's Comb

Novice: Rinsed First
Advanced: Unrinsed but Looks Clean and It's from a Friend
Daredevil: Has Hair or Fuzz in It but Comes from a Friend You Know Is Pretty Clean
Crazy Person: Unrinsed from a Stranger—but Looks Clean
Unrinsed, from a Stranger, with Hair or Fuzz in Evidence (See: "Things We Never Do")

- Using a Staple Gun
- Sitting with Your Mouth Open
- Driving Barefoot
- Walking with Your Hands in Your Pockets (See: "Adventures in Sex")
- Playing Any Sport When It's Too Hot
- Playing Any Sport with Your Shirt Off
- Four or More People on a Three-Person Couch
- Swimming in the Rain
- Walking Around with Your Shoelaces Untied
- Bouncing a Ball in the House
- Pointing
- Riding a Vacuum Cleaner

Adventures in Stairs

Novice: Going Upstairs Two at a Time
Crazy Person: Going Downstairs Two at a Time

Adventures in Swimming

Novice: Swimming Underwater
Advanced: Without Nose Clips
Daredevil: With Your Eyes Open
Crazy Person: In a Public Pool

- Swimming Less Than an Hour after Eating

- Roller Skating on a Rug
- Standing Up in a Rowboat
- Spinning Around Until You Get Nauseous and Dizzy and Fall Down
- Getting Nauseous and Dizzy and Falling Down Without Spinning Around First
- Ironing with Wet Hands
- Walking with a Toothpick in Your Mouth

Adventures in Business

Adventures in Taxes

Novice: Hiring an Unrecommended Accountant to Do the Short Form
Advanced: Hiring an Unrecommended Accountant to Do the Long Form
Daredevil: Doing the Short Form Yourself
Crazy Person: Doing the Long Form Yourself

Adventures in Calling Your Boss by His or Her First Name Before He or She Tells You To

Novice: When You're Both Drunk and Out of Town on a Business Trip
Advanced: When You're Both Drunk at an Office Party
Daredevil: In the John
Crazy Person: In a Meeting

- Picking Your Nose with Your Office Door Open (See "Adventures in Sports")
- Not Wearing a Belt (See: All Other Categories)
- Wearing Your Casual Clothes to the Office

  Crazy Person: If You Work on Wall Street

- Carrying Money Loose Without Using a Wallet
- Attending a Meeting Without a Pen

Adventures in Job Hunting

Novice: Applying for a Job Without an MBA Degree
Advanced: Applying for a Job with an Honest Résumé
Daredevil: Applying for a Job with a Doctored Résumé
Crazy Person: Applying for a Job with an Ex-Lover's or Spouse's Company

- Waiting to Pay Your Insurance Premium Until the Grace Period
- Working Freelance

Adventures with the Typewriter

Novice: Typing Without Looking at the Keys
Daredevil: Changing Your Own Typewriter Ribbon
Advanced: Not Proofreading What You Type
Crazy Person: Continuing to Type After You Hear the Margin Bell

Adventures with Tools

- Taking Bread Out of a Toaster with a Fork
- Fixing a Flat

Adventures in Assembling Things

Novice: Up to Two Parts, with Instructions
Advanced: Up to Two Parts, Without Instructions
Daredevil: Three or More Parts, with or Without Instructions
Crazy Person: Anything That Has to Be Plugged In

- Putting in a Thumbtack with Your Bare Hands
- Using a Knife for Anything Besides Cutting Food
- Picking Your Teeth with a Fork
- Opening a Bobby Pin with Your Teeth
- Defrosting the Refrigerator with a Sharp Instrument Instead of Waiting for the Ice to Melt
- Drying Your Clothes on the Radiator
- Not Using a Cutting Board
- Checking Your Own Oil

Crazy Person: With the Engine Running

- Using the Self-Service Pump at a Gas Station
- Hanging a Picture by Yourself

Daredevil: While Using a Push-Button Tape Measure
Potential Hazards: Whiplash, Severe Lacerations, and Concussion

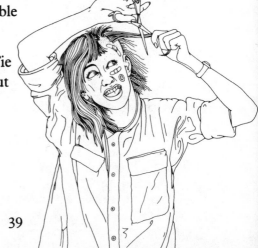

- Sewing Without a Thimble (See: "Adventures in Sports")
- Tying Your Own Bow Tie
- Giving Yourself a Haircut

39

Adventures with Power Tools

Novice: Owning a Power Tool
Advanced: Using a Power Tool
Daredevil: Using a Power Tool After It's Been Plugged In

Adventures in Media and the Arts

- Going to a Movie by Yourself
- Calling a Talk Show with the Radio On
- Whistling in a Crowded Elevator
- Listening to Your Walkman with the Volume in the Red Zone

Daredevil: Singing Alone—Out Loud—in Public!

- Making Faces

Warning 1: You could get caught. (*Note:* The Commodore doesn't believe this is a warning. He believes this is an essential part of the thrill.)

Warning 2: Your face could stay that way. (*Note:* The Doctor believes *this* is an essential part of the thrill. Hey, no pain, no gain!)

Warning 3: This does not include going cross-eyed. (See: "Ultimate Adventures: Tempting the Devil")

- Playing an Electric Guitar with a Wet Head
- Wearing Loud Shoes in a Museum
- Wearing Long Underwear to an Indoor Concert
- Sneaking Food to Your Seat at the Philharmonic

Daredevil: Swallowing Loudly

Adventures in Health and Medicine

- Not taking Dramamine Before a Trip
- Giving Yourself an Enema (See: "Adventures in Sports" and "Adventures with Tools")
- Taking Your Clothes off in Front of Your Doctor
- Taking Your Clothes off in Front of Your Nurse
- Picking at a Scab
- Showering with a Cold
- Rubbing Your Eyes When They Itch
- Going Without Underwear

  Wearing Jockey Shorts to Bed (See "Things We Never Do")
  Potential Hazards: Growth of Moss; Hormonal Imbalance; Public Humiliation; Suicide

  Wearing a Bra to Bed (See: "Things We Never Do")
  Potential Hazards (See "Wearing Jockey Shorts to Bed")

- Sleeping in a Loft Bed

  Warning: Leads to Constant Nosebleeds and Nausea
  Other Potential Hazards: Vertigo; Giddiness; Falling and Driving Nose into Your Brain

- Sleeping Without a Pillow

  Potential Hazards: Leads to Soft Spots

- Eating a Full Meal Before Going to the Dentist
- Taking a Pill Without Using Water

   Potential Hazards: Asphyxiation, Leading to Emergency Tracheotomy; in Struggle to Dislodge Pill from Throat, Capsule Could Be Propelled into Cranium at High Speed

- Swallowing More Than One Pill at a Time

   Potential Hazards: Could Permanently Stretch the Inside of Your Throat, Causing Excruciating Pain When Wearing a Bow Tie

Adventures in Knuckle-Cracking

Novice: The Big Knuckles
Advanced: The Finger Joints
Daredevil: Toes
Crazy Person: Neck, Ankle, Wrist, or Other

- Brushing Your Teeth in the Kitchen Sink
- Not Taking Your Temperature When You're Too Sick to Go to Work or School
- Wearing a Radium Dial Watch

   Tragic Warning: Has Been Known to Cause Genitals to Turn Green and Make a Whistling Noise

- Sitting Too Close to the Television (See: "Tragic Warning" above)
- Wearing Synthetic Fibers
- Wearing a Strapless Bra for the First Time

   Crazy Person: If You're Larger Than a C Cup or Smaller Than an A

- Wearing Makeup to Bed

   Potential Hazards: Aging; Loss of Eyelashes; Tragic Loss of Collagen

- Reading in a Bad Light
- Not Sitting Up Straight
- Wearing a Band-Aid or Bandage Too Tight
- Using Locker Room Soap or Shampoo
- Waxing Your Legs Without a Local Anesthesia

Adventures in School and Youth

- Graduating from High School with Your Natural Nose

For Parents Only

Daredevil: Applying to Kindergarten Only One Year in Advance
Crazy Person: Applying to Private School on Child's Merits Alone

- Not Using Reinforcements
- Volunteering for Hall Monitor
- Showing Up at School in Boy Scout or Girl Scout Uniform
- Attending Boy/Girl Party Wearing a Night Brace
- Not Applying to Boston, Syracuse, George Washington, or Any Florida Universities
- Dating Someone Who Lives in Your Dorm
- Majoring in Liberal Arts
- Signing Up for the Full Meal Plan
- Stealing Silverware from the Cafeteria
- Depending on the Ride Board to Get Home for Thanksgiving
- Taking Organic Chem from an Oriental Professor
- Sleeping with Your Ex's Roommate
- Getting a Gynecological Exam at Health Services

- Taking the SAT, GRE, GMAT, or LSAT Without a Preparatory Course
- Not Going into Father's Business
- Going to a Sleep-Away College
- Cleaning the Erasers Indoors

Adventures in Defiance

- Acting Up in Front of Company

Potential Hazards: Inability to Stop
Can Lead to Hyperventilation, Insanity, and Social
Ostracism; Company Might Experience Cardiac
Infarction

- Talking Back
- Asking Strangers to be Quiet in a Movie Theater
- Biting Your Nails in Front of Company
- Pointing and Staring (See: "Adventures in Sports")
- Closing the Door to Your Room (See: "Adventures in Sex")
- Putting Your Feet on the Furniture
- Talking or Eating Loudly in a Library

Potential Hazard: Prison Record

- Staying Up Too Late
- Changing Plans at the Last Minute
- Removing the Collar Stays from Your Shirt

Potential Hazard: Blindness

- Not Tucking in Your Shirt
- Eating Anything in Bed When You're Not Sick
- Wearing an Old Bra
- Leaving the Lights On When You're in Another Room
- Going to the Bathroom, Taking a Shower, or Going to the Incinerator Without Turning Your Phone Machine On

Adventures in Dating

Novice: Going on a Date with Someone You Know
First Class: Going on a Date with Someone Who Likes You
Daredevil: Going on a Date With Someone You Like
Crazy Person: Going on a Second Date With Someone You Like Who Likes You
(*Warning:* This Could Lead to Something)

- Allowing Your Girlfriend or Boyfriend to Go Out to Dinner With Her or His Old Boyfriend or Girlfriend
- Going on a Double Date with Your Boss and His or Her Spouse
- Going to a Restaurant That Doesn't Accept Credit Cards

Adventures in Ordering Cheese Fondue

Daredevil: Without Using Napkins
Crazy Person: Wearing Your Good Pants or Shoes

- Wearing Old Underpants on a Date
- Introducing Yourself to Your Date's Parents Before They Know About You
- Not Going Through Your New Date's Medicine Cabinet
- Swallowing
- Buying a Queen-Size Bed (or Larger) While Single

Warning: If Male, the Wrong Element Will Be Attracted to You. If Female, This Will Put a Curse on Entire Future Social Life.

Adventures in Birth Control

Novice: Carrying Your Diaphragm in Your Purse
Advanced: Not Carrying Your Diaphragm in Your Purse
Daredevil: Carrying Your Purse in Your Diaphragm

The Jewish Adventurers' Blind Date

Here, for all beginners yearning to cut their romantic teeth in an adventurous way, is the classic, blind JAC date.

He: Leaves the house without full breath-saving artillery: Tic Tac, Binaca spray, Certs, and Odor Eaters in shoes.

She: Arranges date the same day she has a major hair renovation by unknown hairdresser.

He: Decides against going to cash machine first.

She: Does not answer the door in stocking feet; wears three-inch heels without knowing height of date.

He: Does not make restaurant reservations in advance.

She: Does not admit to hating Chinese food.

He: Doesn't ask what's in "the Garden of Earthly Delights."

She: Doesn't say "Hold the MSG."

He: Eats with chopsticks.

She: Doesn't check herself out in a mirror three times during the meal.

He: Asks for doggy bag.

She: Doesn't offer to pay her half of the check.

He: Asks if he can take her home.

She: Says yes.

He: Asks if he can use the john.

She: Doesn't check first to see if Tampax are hidden.

He: Says he had a nice evening without thinking of the consequences.

She: Says "Me too," ignoring humiliation of doggy bag.

He: Says he wants to kiss her.

She: Does not issue medical questionnaire, prepared for just such emergencies by her physician father.

He: Kisses her.

She: Kisses back with her lips slightly parted.

He: Mentions he loves children.

She: Offers her tongue.

He: Gives her his home phone number.

She: Calls her parents, who call the caterers, the minister, the justice of the peace, or the Ayatollah.

Ultimate Adventures: Tempting the Devil

Warning: No Novices, Please. These Are Extremely Dangerous Adventures. We Can't Caution You Enough.

Adventures in Walking

Advanced: Walking Around in Socks but No Slippers
Daredevil: Walking Around the House in Bare Feet
Crazy Person: Walking Barefoot on a Boardwalk
(*Warning:* Germs Could Get into Hangnail on Toe and Spread Through Bloodstream. Could Lead to Paralysis, Death, or Worse.)
Walking Around in Untied Shoes (See: "Things We Never Do")

- Thinking About Getting Tattooed
- Giving Advice
- Stretching or Playing with the Telephone Cord

  Potential Hazards: Strangulation; Dizziness

- Picking at or Unraveling a Wicker Chair at a Stranger's House
- Sleeping Sitting Up
- Going Too Close to the Edge
- Referring to Your Mother in Your Father's Presence as "Her" or "She"
- Talking to a Policeman
- Tearing Open a Candy Package with Your Teeth
- Shaking Hands with Someone Who Has a Cold

Adventures in Dancing

Advanced: Dancing Crazy or Wild in the House
Daredevil: At a Party
Crazy Person: Alone

Adventures in Windows

Daredevil: Opening a Stuck Window With Your Bare Hands
Crazy Person: Above the Third Floor
(*Potential Hazard:* Loss of Memory)

- Opening a Carton with Your Bare Hands
- Writing on Your Skin with a Pen or Pencil
- Looking Cross-Eyed
- Not Calling Your Parents for Three Months
- Wearing Anything Lighter Than Dark Brown When You Have Your Period

Adventures in Smoking

Advanced: Lighting Your Cigarette From a Candle
Daredevil: From a Stove
Crazy Person: From a Bonfire

- Taking a Scissors from Someone with the Point Edge Facing You
- Do-Si-Do-ing Without a Partner
- Sitting in the Front Row of a Balcony
- Eating Something That Was Dropped on the Floor
- Daring to Be Late
- Drinking out of a Stranger's Glass
- Not Putting on a Sweater When Your Mother Is Cold
- Swallowing Watermelon Seeds

Over the Edge
A Warning on What Can Happen if You Go Too Far

We realize that one danger of publishing this book is that people might think of JAC activities as nothing but glamorous, sexy, or even frivolous adventures.

Nothing could be further from the truth! Except the sexy part.

Beware, future Adventurers! Don't go sitting around the house in a wet bathing suit just because you think it will help you meet members of the opposite sex! There are too many things that can go wrong. Would you treat sky-diving lightly? Would you tame a lion without a whip? Of course not. So why blow bubbles in your chocolate milk without proper preparation? Why use locker room soap or shampoo without knowing the inherent dangers?

The JAC is, above all, a responsible organization. We believe in four things: Knowledge, Preparation, Insurance, and Proper Equipment (see "The Official JAC Catalog" and receive official JAC 20 percent discount).

Beware: Too many members have already crossed the line to the point of no return. These are the people you see sneaking into Chinese restaurants for their daily fix of MSG, going out after nine o'clock at night to drink caffeinated coffee—during the week—and taking car trips of over an hour without bringing along a Thermos of either ice water or diet soda. Yes, Adventure can be your life, but you don't want to end up with a nickname like Shakey, Twitchy, Blinkey, Stumpy, or Soup Brain. You don't want to wind up like Lars Petselou! (*See next page.*)

The Story of Lars Petselou

Lars Petselou had it all: a nice wife, a family, a thriving zipper-repair business. He also managed to include a healthy degree of Adventure into his life. But he got cocky, went off half-cocked, and began to engage in one Adventure after another, willy nilly.

One day, he cut his toenails in bed. Then, without washing his hands first, he ate a leftover tuna sandwich that had been in the refrigerator unwrapped since lunchtime. He sat panting and staring at the pile of toenail clippings and crumbs on the sheets and suddenly realized that he had gone over the edge.

And he also knew it was too late. The excitement and thrill he was feeling in his sinuses, with the rush of fluids and all, would now be impossible to do without. He pushed the button on the Official JAC Vacuum Sheet and watched the nail clippings and crumbs get sucked away, along with his self-respect. He kissed his drooling dog on the lips, then walked into the cold winter night without a belt.

Before long he had become a man who didn't send thank-you notes and who wiped his nose on his sleeve.

He is now a raving lunatic.

WORKS OF ART CREATED BY
JAC MEMBERS

BOOKS:

All Our Heads Were Wet
Ring Around My Seat
A House Is Not a Home
Chance and Me
Yes, Maybe, I Think I Can!
If the Suit Fits, Tear It
The Schmuck Who Skied Everest:
A Critical Analysis
Don't Put Off That Tracheotomy!

MOVIES:

The Magnificent Minyan
The High and the Nauseous
The Big Draft
Citizen Weinburg
Passing the Stone

TV SERIES:

The Young and
the Nauseous
The Wild,
Wild Vest

SONGS:

Gloves Make the World Go Round
Our Gloves Are Here to Stay
The Surrey with the Splash Guard
on Top
I'm Getting Overheated Over You
Standing Up in a Rowboat
Watching All the Girls Go By
I'll Get By As Long As
I Have Shoes
I've Got the World in a Sling
I've Got Plenty O'Roughage

Dare to Be Late
The Official JAC Song

(How Can You Love a Wild Man?)

Dweedeedeep do da da do da da da do da
Dweedeedeep do da da do da da da do da
Dweedeedeep do da da do da da da do da dweep do dee dee do
                                                                      dee do deep

Dare to be late
Hey what's the hurry
Dare to be late
Now don't you worry
Dare to be late
How can you love a wild man?

I eat up all the bread before dinner
I go swimmin' then I sit around
On the subway I freefall like a winner
You know what, baby? I don't fall down
(He don't fall down, no!)

Dare to be late
I'm just so lazy
Dare to be late
I make you crazy
Dare to be late
How can you love a wild man?

I stand right next to the window if it's high up
If you tickle me I'll never smile
I can walk around the house with my eyes shut
Look at me, baby, I'm mister style
(He's mister style, Yes he is!)

First Refrain

I'll lean back in my chair if you scold me
I'll go walking when my head is still wet
I'm so silly you know you can't hold me
Hey, babe, I'm in the danger set
(He sure is, yeah!)

Second Refrain

He don't fall down
He's in the danger set
He goes to town
He gets his head all wet
He don't fall down
He's in the danger set
How can you love a wild man?

Dare to be late!

An excerpt from the world-famous novel by the greatest J.A.C. writer who ever lived, the man who Ernest Hemingway referred to as "that guy, what's his name, the one who kept putting the fish hook through his finger."

The Sun Overslept

by Marco Herring

A JAC PUBLICATION
NEW YORK

Chapter Three

It was 10:30 P.M. Silly hour. Damned ridiculous time to be awake. And for what? She wasn't here anyway. I leaned out over the balcony and took a long look at the city. Lights flashed on and off down there while little cars took little people in big circles through a maze of streets, spinning and darting and flashing lots of colors like flares going off in all directions. I was beginning to get a little nauseous. Enough was enough. I unhooked the nose strap, unsnapped the neckpiece, and let the harness fall behind me. I took the cotton out of my ears, stepped out of the weighted boots, and sort of strolled inside. What the hell. I'd have another look later.

There was a knock at the door. I answered, and Hoyt Schermerhorn stuck his nubby little head in. His eyes bugged out at me, swollen from trying to hang on to a sinus headache. Flecks of seeded rye from a recent round robin covered his cheeks. He was out of control.

"Hey, Rake. Hey, Rake! Wanna come?"

"Where?" I shot back, strangely specific for me.

"We're all going up to Rayburn's. He's gonna act up in front of his aunt."

13

Marco Herring

"How does he know she'll be there?" I'd hurt him. You could see it. I didn't mean to. "Sorry, Hoyt. It's just not for me, I guess."

"He's gonna wear a thick belt."

"Sorry."

The door slammed, and he was gone. Confused, I guess.

I dropped my pants and looked in the mirror. It was such a silly wound, a damned silly one, but real. Who'd have thought that melted chocolate could do that to a man? That day came into focus. It had been a cloudy one, rain imminent, a perfect one for our breed. You could usually find us on the Right Bank in those days, sort of stirring around. That particular afternoon I was eating a chocolate crepe with no napkin—pushing the limits, so to speak. A few lovely young admirers giggled behind me. They followed us everywhere. Cute ones with bad teeth. Tempting, but I was focused on the action.

A circle was forming around Katz and Fontana. They were giving each other nuggies. Innocent enough, but everyone knew that knobboes were just a step away. I saw Claire stalking away from the circle in tears. I guess she'd been with Katz too long to stand it anymore. I moved toward her. That's when it happened. The crepe came apart, and the chocolate poured all over my front. By the time I got to her, my chest was covered with the stuff.

"Rake! Look at you! Here, use this." She held out her handkerchief. I didn't notice. I was staring down at the stuff on me. Then a light went on.

"No, thanks, really. I think I'll keep it."

Her eyes widened in horror.

"Keep it? Keep it!" she shrieked. "My God! Get away from me. You're just like the rest of them."

14

THE SUN OVERSLEPT

"Hey, look, I kept a hangnail past Christmas. What's a chestful of chocolate?" A chestful, sure, but who knew that stuff could travel? I didn't.

A second door slam brought me back, and there she was in front of me. She was so damned beautiful, with her face flushed red. She was overheated, the silly kid, but she didn't know it. She wasn't wearing a gauge.

"Hello, darling. Sorry I'm late. I was out with a friend."

And who was it this time? I tortured myself with the question. Was it Pascal, the hill roller? Gene, the tunnel yeller? Or maybe even Sven, the skinny kid who did things with his shirt off?

"Can I have a kiss?"

"No. Stay away."

"No saliva, I promise."

"No, really."

"I heard you caused quite a row the other day."

"I guess."

"How's Katz?"

"Pretty bad. He may not make it."

"What is it?"

"Pink belly."

"God. Can I have a hug?"

"No, I told you."

"Why not?"

"Because." She wasn't listening. Just looking down.

"Wow! Slipper socks!"

Damn, I forgot about those. True, they were provocative, but I didn't want to be a tease. But then it didn't matter. Not now. No. Not anymore.

"Wanna go for a ride with the windows up?"

Her voice was beginning to fade. The next day was

15

pulling at me. I killed the lights, stretched out, and had a wrestling match with my pillow.

"Wanna gulp down some milk?" I could hear her off in the corner somewhere, still damned beautiful in the pitch black.

"Rake? I got one."

"What?"

"We could untuck our shirts; then we could spin around till we get nauseous and fall down; in a boat maybe; then we could eat a full meal and wake up Serge the dentist. You'd do it if you loved me. I know you would."

Call me a coward, a fool, whatever, but I had to answer her.

"Yes, yes I know. Isn't it pretty to think so?"

About the Author

Marco Herring, born near a nice park, was educated in public schools, where he served as a hall monitor during the Spanish Civil War. After graduation he traveled a lot and killed himself when he deliberately tried to make it through a revolving door with his shirt untucked.

It's a little-known fact that Raymond Chandler used to baby-sit for the young Chance Weinburg. Chance, even at the tender age of three, so inspired America's most hard-boiled writer that Chandler carried the memory of the incorrigible youth with him until the day he died. This is an excerpt from Chandler's last, unfinished manuscript, which many scholars feel is heavily influenced by the author's encounters with our founder.

THE LONG GESCHREI

Chapter One

It was a crummy winter day, and I was sitting in my crummy downtown office when she walked into my crummy life. Suddenly things weren't so crummy anymore. How could they be when dames wore sweaters that tight? I wondered if she was worried what that did to her circulation. But she was a big girl. She could take care of herself.

My desk was in the direct sunlight, so I was wearing plenty of zinc oxide on my nose. I offered her some, but she declined with the sweetest smile this side of Sara Lee.

"I have a problem," she said.

"I solve problems," I told her, and flashed my own smile, letting her see that I had never worn braces. I leaned backward in my chair, balancing myself on the back two legs. The look in her eye told me she was impressed. After a few seconds, I eased myself down slowly so all four legs were touching the floor. I'd felt a

1

nosebleed coming, and she looked like her life was messy enough.

"It's my sister," she began, but she started to tremble. If she was the trembling type, then I was the kind of guy who'd use thongs in my health club's shower room. But I decided to play along with her game.

"Would you like a cup of coffee?" I asked.

"Do you have decaf?"

I gave her the kind of leer I usually save for when I eat too loudly in a library. "What's the matter? Afraid what'll happen if you stay up past ten?"

"Have it your way," she said, almost sadly.

The kettle was already boiling. Forgoing the hot mitt, I picked it up and poured.

"You'll get a blister!" she screamed. "Get a Band-Aid!"

"I don't keep *Band-Aids* here," I said as evenly as I could manage.

That's when she started to cry and told me she'd killed Terry Lennox.

The Official JAC Catalog

Haberdashers, Outfitters, Suppliers

"Safety is our first, middle, and last name."

The JAC Elements of Style: A Dress Code for the Would-Be Adventurer

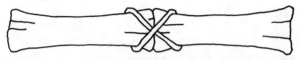

You'll Glow with That Look of Danger If You Wear:

For Men

1. A Tank Top or a Shirt With Your Collar Up
2. Some Sort of Foreign Hat
3. Dirty White Bucks
4. Taps on Your Regular Shoes
5. A Wide Belt (Unless You Wear No Belt)
6. A Lanyard with a Whistle
7. Anything with a Hole in It
8. Your Sleeves Rolled Up
9. Footpads

For Women

1. Support Hose
2. Shoes with Straps or Wedges
3. A Base Coat for Your Nails
4. Some Sort of Foreign Kerchief
5. An Ace Bandage or a Sling
6. Footpads
7. JAC Utility Belt
8. Jumpsuit

JAC Adventure and Travel Log

- A must for all members of our club. Each page comes with invisible carbons and extra pages for legal purposes.
- Includes scratch test and allergy record, vaccination guide, organ donation page, plus many other features.
- $14.95

Pre-Moistened Bathing Suit

- Perfect for the Sitting-Around-in-a-Wet-Bathing Suit Adventurer
- Have the Adventure without the bother of going into the water
- Ready for action when you are
- One size fits all
- $10.00(men's); $30.00 (women's)

Book-a-Like

- For the beginning Going-to-the-Bathroom-Without-Something-to-Read Adventurer
- Looks and feels just like a real book *but can't be opened!*
- $17.95 (hardcover); $3.95 (paperback)

Pocket Combo Pencil Sharpener/ Nasal Inhaler

- When the pencil-running action is fast, you can't afford to stuff up
- Very handy for the Pencil-Running Adventurer with a sinus condition
- $4.95 (Add $2.95 for a dozen official JAC "Sure Grip" number two pencils)

Keep-Fresh Bread Rack

- Ideal for the proud Filling-Up-on-Bread Adventurer
- Plenty of room to display all your favorite loaves (Yes, it *will* hold challah and seeded rye. It even has room for a couple of hard rolls.)
- $22.50
- Croissant Ring available ($2.95)

Used Combs

- Guaranteed to have been used at least once by a total stranger
- $1.99 (fluff and scuzz included)
- *Warning:* Not for Novices!

Porno Movie Hat

- Wide brim, unisex fedora
- Comes with detachable veil and lifelike facial mask guaranteed to make you un-recognizable even to your-self
- Comes in brown and camouflage
- Moistureproof and shockproof
- Versatile; can also be worn to the opera, depending on how you feel about the opera
- $69.00

Power Tool Noises

- Available on 45, LP, tape, and compact discs
- Call for latest prices

Survival Ball-Point Pen

- Contains extra buttons; dental floss; miniature photos of Martin Milner, Robbie Benson, and Sophia Loren; a shoelace; one dose of official JAC Bowel Binding Agent; two safety pins; one toothpick; plastic spoon; thermometer; three tissues
- Exact duplicate of the one carried by "Si" Stallone in the blockbuster film *Rambo:* First Sneeze
- $42.00

Used Drinking Glasses

- Comes in attractive set of six
- Guaranteed different stain per glass
- Stains include: lipstick, fingerprints, food specks, and general smudges
- Affidavit included
- Imported from some of the finest bus terminals in the United States and Europe
- $44.00

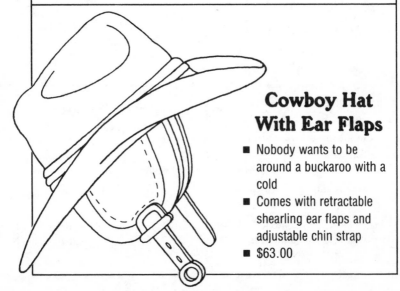

Cowboy Hat With Ear Flaps

- Nobody wants to be around a buckaroo with a cold
- Comes with retractable shearling ear flaps and adjustable chin strap
- $63.00

Leaf Toilet Paper

- 1,000 sheets per roll
- Each sheet shaped exactly like a leaf
- Gets you psychologically prepared for the real thing
- Available in oak ($5.95) and maple ($6.95) only

Training-Chair Legs

- For the Novice Leaning-Back-in-Your-Chair Adventurer
- An extra two legs that attach to the rear of any straight-back chair
- Learn the thrill of leaning back without unnecessary anxiety
- *Special:* Order before Xmas and receive a $20.00 rebate that can be used to pay your superintendent to assemble
- $69.99

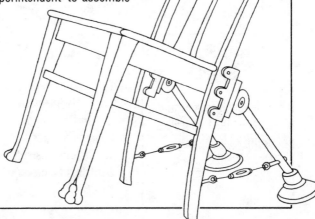

Splinter Scanning Cap

- The newest in high-tech warning devices that can help you prevent little wooden slivers from becoming a permanent part of your body
- Scanning range of five hundred feet
- Stroll and explore the world of wood in safety
- $69.95

Solar-Powered Digital Item Counter

- For Supermarket-Express-Lane Adventurers
- Keeps track of all the items in your basket. No need to rely on memory, which could fail in the heat of action
- Straps to wrist!
- $19.95

Skipping Skull Protector

- A cautious foam rubber cushion for the serious skipper
- Attaches comfortably to the back of your head (surgical attachment optional)
- Why end your conscious days with an unexpected back slide?
- Comes in colors and shapes; can be customized to resemble a hat or a funny little animal friend
- $14.95 (Add $10.00 for surgical attachment; add $15.00 for camel shape)

Untuckable Shirt

- Scientific breakthrough! Guaranteed impossible to tuck in
- One size fits all badly
- $35.00

Fellatio Mittens

- Even the devil himself could not penetrate these lead-lined sexy instruments of love. Say hello and hang on in your own special way with a touch as soft as that of Santa's little helpers.
- $15.00

Bathroom Video

- Complete step-by-step instructions from showering without a mat to shaving with a used blade
- Everything you need to know about the most important room in the house!
- Put together by world-renowned bathroom triathlete Yvette "Squeeze" Montand
- $49.95 ($59.95 for Beta)

Speedy Rubber Glove Extensions

- For female adventurers with fake nails
- Extenders, with suction cups, for daredevil top-shelf dusting and hot water dishwashing
- Available in three lengths
- $6.95

Strap-On Arm

- For those daredevil Driving-with-Your-Arm-Out-the-Window Adventurers
- Gets you ready for the real thing but lets you hold on to the wheel with both hands
- Comes with rolled-up sleeve
- Looks great for the girls
- $289.50

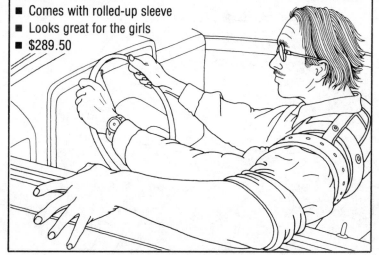

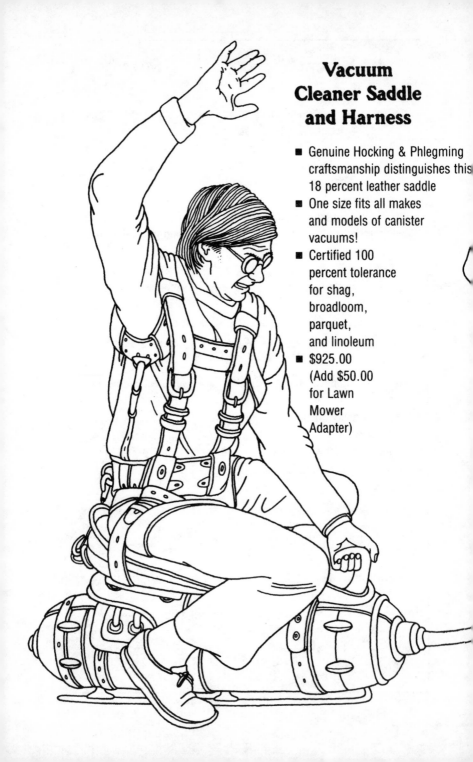

Harnesses
(From Hocking and Phlegming of London, Ltd.)

Specially created and prepared for the JAC by the greatest harness makers in the world, Hocking & Phlegming of London, Ltd., 24¼ Wardour Street, London, England, W2. Over the years, H&P have built harnesses for such notables as Edward, King of England; Charles, Prince of Wales; Charles de Gaulle; Jerry Lewis; and Dwight D. Eisenhower. And now, for the first time, H&P are creating for *you*.

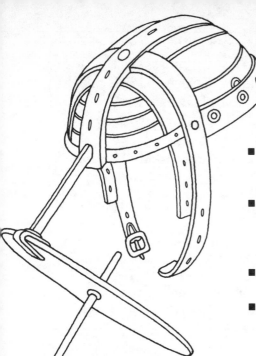

The Official Doctor Seldom Conroy Clip-On Splash Guard

- Fits directly onto your straw and prevents injuries due to exploding bubbles
- Avoid possible eye or brain damage from the number-seventeen killer in America—splashback
- Saves a fortune on cleaning bills
- $6.95
  Be a Crazy Person—
  Don't Be a Stupid Person

The Balcony Harness

- Learn to sit in the front row of any balcony and feel completely secure!
- Easily fastens to the person or persons sitting next to you
- $39.99 (Nasal Inhaler not included)

Subway-Riding Harness

- For the novice Riding-the-Subway-Without-Holding-On Adventurer
- Practice for that moment of free falling! Just fasten to pole, and away you go
- Adjustable
- $49.99

JAC Plasma

- Always good to have a little extra on hand
- All types, from nice families
- $45 per ounce

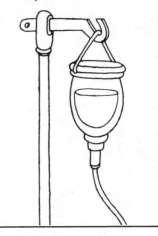

Speed Merkin's Knumb-Knees

- A light, lemon-scented, topical anesthetic designed to desensitize legs. Apply one hour before leg waxing, shaving, or—for the very delicate—applying hose.
- Awaiting FDA approval
- $12.50 (6-ounce bottle); $22.50 (12-ounce bottle)

Vacuum Sheets

- Amazing, high-tech, computerized, and Sanforized: eat in bed without napkins, trays, bibs, or anxiety
- Suck up crumbs with the touch of a button

$175.95 (twin) $200.00 (queen) $300.00 (king)

Kite-Flying Goggles

- Because those things could come crashing down from God knows how high and poke your eyes out
- $7.95 ($8.95 tinted)

Speed-Reading Dramamine

- Special formula designed to prevent speed-reading sickness
- With a secret memory-protection ingredient!
- Available by the gross only
- $400.00 (With attractive dispenser: $410.00)

Digital Sprinkler Hat

- Looks real snappy!
- For the Adventurer who wants a wet head when he/she wants it!
- Can be connected to the overheating gauge and is then triggered automatically when the gauge dial enters the red zone!
- Water not included
- $29.95 (With 800 feet of special rubber hose: $495.00)

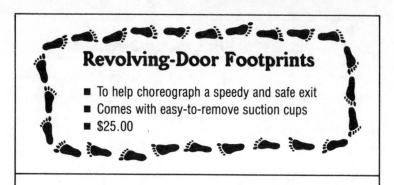

Revolving-Door Footprints

- To help choreograph a speedy and safe exit
- Comes with easy-to-remove suction cups
- $25.00

JAC Designer Wristwatch
and Overheating Gauge

- Permanently set fifteen minutes behind. For all Adventurers whose specialty is daring to be late, or not unbuttoning their coats
- Comes in Rolex, Tank, and Mod black styling
- Recommended for both men and women during sex
- $250.00

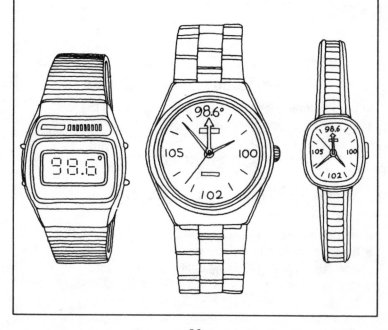

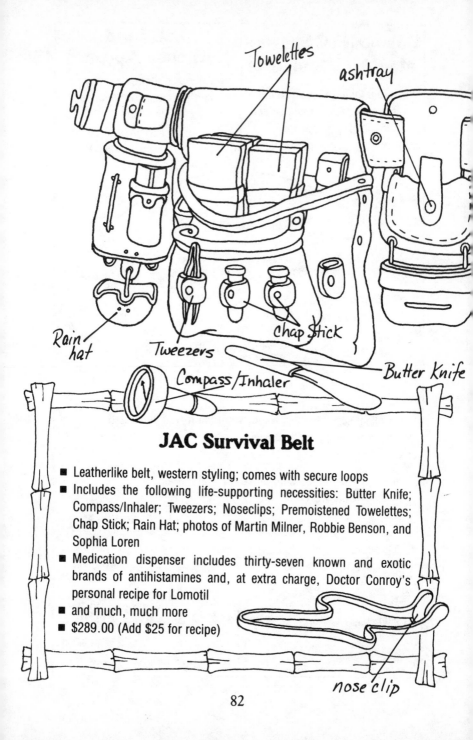

Towelettes

ashtray

Rain hat

Tweezers

Compass/Inhaler

chap stick

Butter Knife

nose clip

JAC Survival Belt

- Leatherlike belt, western styling; comes with secure loops
- Includes the following life-supporting necessities: Butter Knife; Compass/Inhaler; Tweezers; Noseclips; Premoistened Towelettes; Chap Stick; Rain Hat; photos of Martin Milner, Robbie Benson, and Sophia Loren
- Medication dispenser includes thirty-seven known and exotic brands of antihistamines and, at extra charge, Doctor Conroy's personal recipe for Lomotil
- and much, much more
- $289.00 (Add $25 for recipe)

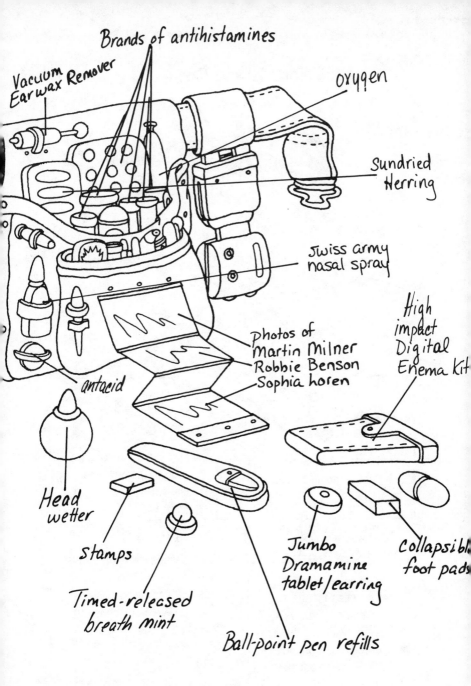

Brands of antihistamines

Vacuum Earwax Remover

oxygen

Sundried Herring

Swiss army nasal spray

Photos of Martin Milner Robbie Benson Sophia Loren

High impact Digital Enema Kit

antacid

Head wetter

stamps

Timed-released breath mint

Jumbo Dramamine tablet/earring

Collapsibl foot pads

Ball-point pen refills

Ascot/Neck Brace Combo

- For the Kite-Flying Adventurer
- Look sharp, be safe!
- $24.95

Cheese Fondue Slicker

- Comes in American, Swiss, and Camembert colors
- $19.95

Amplifier Socks

- Just like the gloves, only you put them on your feet!
- $479.95

Official JAC Good Pants

- You've never played base-ball or eaten fondue in good pants till you've played or eaten in these
- $200.00 (blue Gabardine)
  $225.00 (charcoal gray flannel)

No-Belt

- Clear plastic belt that is almost invisible
- Ideal for the pre-Novice Not-Wearing-a-Belt Adventurer in training
- $15.95   ↓

→

belt actually shown

JAC Walkie-Talkie

- When you go to the bathroom without something to read, don't go without this!
- Give the other receiver to your best buddy—you never know when someone will have to break the door down and come get you
- $49.95

Number Two on the Town

- A complete guide to public toilets around the world
- Water and shock resistant!
- $15.95

Un-lacing Shoelaces

- Scientific breakthrough from the inventor of the untuckable shirt
- Guaranteed to unlace at some time during the day
- No need to bend over and do it yourself, so you can't throw your back out
- $12.95 (black); $16.95 (brown); doesn't come in white

Amplifier Gloves

- Ideal for the Knuckle-Cracking Adventurer who is hard of hearing or who just likes the big knuckle sound!
- Available with speakers or headphones, AC/DC, lined or unlined
- Extension speakers also available
- $479.95

Bread Loader

- Fend off the main course with one hand and wave with another while these mechanical hands stuff you with a baker's dozen
- Speed and pressure fully adjustable
- Portable; battery operated; comes in attractive attaché case
- $250.00

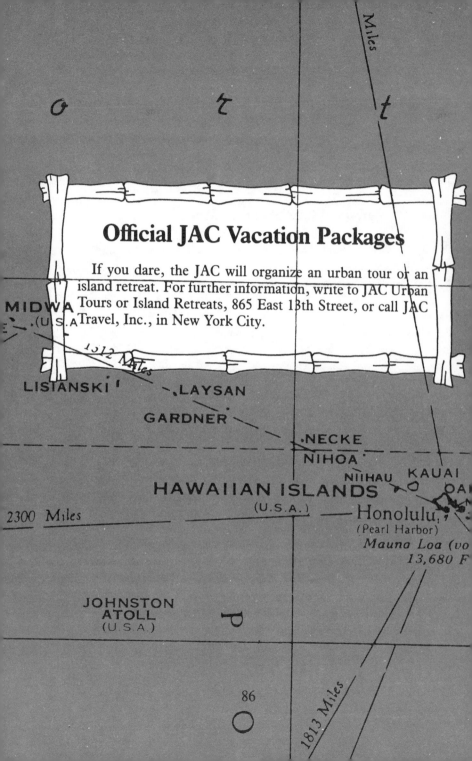

Official JAC Vacation Packages

If you dare, the JAC will organize an urban tour or an island retreat. For further information, write to JAC Urban Tours or Island Retreats, 865 East 13th Street, or call JAC Travel, Inc., in New York City.

MIDWA
.(U.S.A

Miles

t

o

z

t

1512 Miles

LISIANSKI   ,LAYSAN

GARDNER -

,NECKE
NIHOA

NIIHAU   KAUAI

HAWAIIAN ISLANDS   O   OA

(U.S.A.)

2300 Miles   Honolulu,
(Pearl Harbor)
Mauna Loa (vo
13,680 F

JOHNSTON
ATOLL
(U.S.A.)

P

86

O

1813 Miles

h

Expedition to Hawaii

- Eat an airport nacho before takeoff—yum!
- Don't check on the weather first. Yikes!
- Don't waste time buying sun protection, prescription drugs, or sanitary products here; you can always do that when you arrive! (Or *can* you?)
- Stay at accommodations that don't have chain locks on the doors!
- Rely on the front desk to confirm your return flight!
- Buy a sarong: it looks great on you!
- Eat on the beach without a beach towel or blanket!
- Sit around a fire on the beach at night!
- Go swimming in the hotel pool at night!
- Walk near the ocean at night!
- Dance the hula on stage with a fat lady with a gold tooth.
- Go swimming less than an hour after eating a piece of pineapple!
- Open a coconut with a machete!
- Stand up in an outrigger canoe!
- Eat unknown foods with your fingers!
- Lean back in a porch chair!
- Don't wash your feet after coming in from the beach!
- Wear a bathing suit in the lobby!
- Watch a man wearing a handkerchief for shorts throw a torch in the air!
- Join the zany Wet Posture Contest. That's right—everyone has to get hosed down and stand up completely straight for at least five minutes!
- Enjoy "Tappy Hour"—drink the native water in exotic cocktails or even *straight from the tap!*

AI
UI
Hilo
AWAII

c

cisco 4215 Miles

Safari to London

This is for the very experienced Adventurer *only!* Don't even *try* to fake your Adventuring credentials. You must have the heart of a lion, nerves of steel, and a doctor's note!

Features:

- A breathtakingly risky ride to the airport on *public* transportation (leaving less than two hours before departure!)
- Check in your luggage at the sidewalk—with no luggage tags!
- *Optional:* You may purchase tickets *at the airport*! Or fly standby! (*Note:* These options not available to asthmatics.)
- *Optional:* Take a walk on the wild side—use cash, not traveler's checks

On the Airplane

- Sit in a window seat!
- Reach for your Dramamine—and find your bottle empty!
- Talk to strangers!
- Sleep without a pillow or eyeshades!
- Turn the volume on the movie up *full blast*
- Don't pay full attention when the stewardess explains the safety precautions
- Lavatory Adventure Package available (fully supervised)

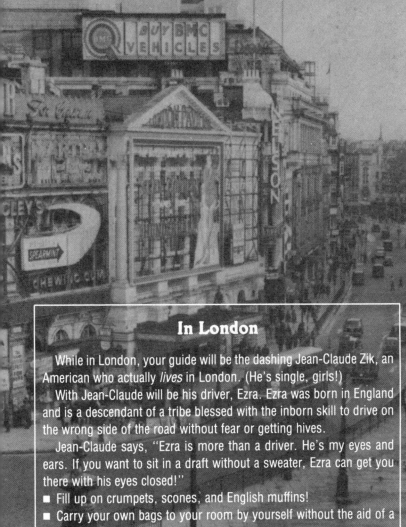

In London

While in London, your guide will be the dashing Jean-Claude Zik, an American who actually *lives* in London. (He's single, girls!)

With Jean-Claude will be his driver, Ezra. Ezra was born in England and is a descendant of a tribe blessed with the inborn skill to drive on the wrong side of the road without fear or getting hives.

Jean-Claude says, "Ezra is more than a driver. He's my eyes and ears. If you want to sit in a draft without a sweater, Ezra can get you there with his eyes closed!"

■ Fill up on crumpets, scones, and English muffins!
■ Carry your own bags to your room by yourself without the aid of a bellhop (map provided)!
■ Share a room with a *total stranger* (same color toothbrushes provided to all roommates)!
■ Feed the pigeons in Hyde Park!
■ Drink warm ale!
■ Go on the *treacherous bad shoes cobblestone trek!* (It's just what it says: a trek in bad shoes on cobblestone streets. Guaranteed to last more than two hours!)

JAC Historical Time Line: A New Perspective on Danger

1492:   Columbus discovers America.

1492:   While in her tepee with the flap open, Princess Sitting Wet-Feathers finds something interesting in her nose.

1903:   The Wright Brothers fly the first powered airplane at Kitty Hawk.

1903:   Kathleen Maloney goes down stairs two at a time in her mother's house in Swampscott, Massachusetts.

1909:   Robert E. Peary reaches the North Pole.

1909:   Leon Nickolaides makes a snowball without using gloves.

1927:   Charles A. Lindbergh flies the monoplane, "Spirit of St. Louis" nonstop from New York to Paris in 33.5 hours.

1927:   Harmon Vone reads *War and Peace* in a bad light, in a draft, lying on the floor, during the hay-fever season.

1937:   Amelia Earhart attempts a flight across the Pacific and disappears.

1937:   Mookathaniel Thang leaves the house without tucking his shirt in and is never seen or heard from again.

1945:   The United States drops the atom bomb on Hiroshima.

1945:   Bob Suede plays catch with his grandmother's china statuette while she's at the movies.

1951:   Bobby Thompson hits the home run "heard 'round the world" to win the National League pennant.

1951:   Spike Spitalowitz plays softball in his good pants.

1953:   Sir Edmund Hilary climbs Mount Everest.

1953:   Sid Fong rides glass elevator on the outside of a hotel to the revolving disco on the top floor. He triumphantly dances a victory dance near a window with an American flag toothpick in his mouth.

1954:   Roger Bannister breaks the four-minute mile.

1954:   A guy named Miles slides down a bannister in short pants.

1969:   Neil Armstrong becomes the first man to walk on the moon.

1969:   Selma Thymus flies standby on a 747 flight from New York to Los Angeles. While over the Grand Canyon, she goes solo into a lavatory without something to read, sits without putting paper down, and does not lock the door. She returns safely to her seat nearly two hours after the seatbelt light comes on.

1979:   Ross Perot invades Iran to retrieve employees from Khomeini's takeover.

1979:   Patty Samuels drives to the Canadian border without her passport.

Things We Never Do

Learn from the tragic case of Lars Petselou as well as others of his ilk.

To help keep you on the right side of risk, here is a list of things that even JAC members would never do:

- Drive in England
- Wear Anything Less Than Number Six Sunblock
  (Reckless abandon is one thing; ruining your summer is another!)
- Go into a Singles' Bar Without Eyeliner
- Use a Bidet
- Pick up a Male Hitchhiker (Causes stab wounds)
- Use an Unrinsed Comb from a Stranger with Hair or Fuzz in Evidence (Causes schizophrenia)
- Own a Pet Monkey
- Kiss a Dog or Cat That's Drooling on the Mouth
- Shave Without Shaving Cream
- Shave with a Straight Razor (May result in loss of ability to swallow)
- Go to Sleep with a Wet Head
- Go Into a Basement Where the Lights Are Broken, Alone, at Night, with No Flashlight
- Eat Unwashed Fruit
- Ask for MSG at a Chinese Restaurant
- Wear Jockey Shorts to Bed
- Wear a Bra to Bed
- Buy Mail-Order Meat
- Jog with an Erection

Official JAC Membership Card

Welcome to a World of Danger!

Front

Fingerprint

_____
Name

_____
Signature

Height: _____

Nickname: _____

Shoe Size: _____

Allergies: _____

Back

Rank	Adventure Performed	Date
Novice	_____	____
Advanced	_____	____
Daredevil	_____	____
Crazy Person	_____	____

Additional Allergies: _____